I0056269

How to Convert Callers into Clients

A Radically Simple Approach
to Convert More
of Your Current Leads
Without Spending a Penny
More on Advertising

Michael DeLon
Harlan Schillinger

Copyright © 2017 Michael DeLon and Harlan Schillinger
All Rights Reserved

This publication is designed to provide accurate and authoritative information
regarding the subject matter contained within. It should be understood that the
author and publisher are not engaged in rendering legal, accounting or other
financial service through this medium. The author and publisher shall not be liable
for your misuse of this material and shall have neither liability nor responsibility to
anyone with respect to any loss or damage caused, or alleged to be caused, directly
or indirectly by the information contained in this book. The author and/or publisher
do not guarantee that anyone following these strategies, suggestions, tips, ideas
or techniques will become successful. If legal advice or other expert assistance is
required, the services of a competent professional should be sought.

All rights reserved. No portion of this book may be reproduced mechanically,
electronically, or by any other means, including photocopying, without written
permission of the author. It is illegal to copy the book, post it to a website, or
distribute it by any other means without permission from the author.

ISBN-13: 978-1-946203-41-0

Expert
Press
www.ExpertPress.net

Table of Contents

The End of the Matter

When Solomon wrote the book of Ecclesiastes, he ended it with these words, "The end of the matter...."

From there he summarized his thoughts and makes his point. For some reason, most books follow this pattern. They build their case and make their "big reveal" in the last chapter.

I'm not going to do that here. You are too busy to wait for the punch-line. My theory is that if this concept is right for you, you'll read the rest of the book. If not, then don't waste your time. There are plenty of other attorneys for whom this concept makes sense – some are in your market.

So here's the entire point of this book, the "end of the matter" so to speak:

> **If You're a Personal Injury Attorney You Can Now**
>
> Convert 3% More Leads and
> Put Over $500,000 in Your Pocket
> Using Your Amazon Bestselling Book
> *Without* Spending More on Advertising

Here's how:

❶ **Publish** an Amazon Bestselling Book.

❷ **Utilize** your book in all of your marketing and advertising.

❸ **Give** your book to every lead you receive.

Do that and you'll **stay in front of your leads longer, convert more leads** to clients, and make **more money** *without* spending another dime on more advertising.

This may be a new concept to you, but not to me.

I've helped others become Amazon Bestselling Authors, use their book to convert leads to clients, and put thousands of dollars in their pocket.

Now it's your turn.

You're spending thousands to make the phone ring.

When it does, do you send materials that make you look like everyone else?

Or do you set yourself apart by sending them your book?

You can choose to continue marketing like you have always done... like everyone else in your market does. Or you can choose to set yourself apart, to differentiate yourself, and to be seen as the expert that your prospects should hire.

How?

By sending every lead a signed copy of your Amazon bestselling book.

Nothing else will set you apart, differentiate you, and help you convert more leads into clients faster than having your own Amazon bestselling book.

It's time for you to break away from the crowd, and put yourself in a category of one. It's time for you to become the Amazon bestselling author of your own book.

Then you'll be able to use your book to convert more leads and earn more money without spending more on advertising.

❧

That's the premise of this book. The remaining chapters explain this concept in more detail. I hope you are as interested in converting more leads and making more money as I am. If you are, then turn the page and keep reading.

Chapter 1.

You Don't Need More Leads

We hear it every week and at every conference we attend. "Business is down. I need more leads."

Our response is the same:

- ➲ How many leads are you generating every month now?

- ➲ How many are you converting to clients?

Those two questions tell us everything we need to know.
These are the facts:
You don't need "more leads."
You need to convert more of the leads you're generating.

Here's the math.

Conversion Ratio	Current	+3%
Calls per month	400	400
Conversion %	20%	23%
# of Cases	80	92
Average NET Fee	$4,500	$4,500
Total Revenue/mo	$360,000	$414,000
Total Revenue/yr	$4,320,000	$4,968,000
Additional Net Profit		**$648,000**

By converting just *3% more* of the leads you're already generating, you'll increase your revenue by thousands of dollars per month—*without* spending more money on advertising to generate "more leads."

If you're like most attorneys, you're playing the same game as everyone else. You're doing things how they've always been done. You set up your practice, ran some ads, got some clients, and have repeated that same process for years.

You've gone to seminars to learn how to "do it better" and get more bang for your buck. Upon returning you implemented one or two concepts, then fell back into your old habit patterns.

Whenever a new social media platform is launched, you're told that you "have to be there or you'll lose out." This hype is what keeps you running on the treadmill and not making progress.

The "shiny object syndrome" is a waste of time and money. Your desire may be good—to reach and serve more people—but your execution is poor because you don't have a solid plan that ties your marketing and message together.

Oh, and every other attorney in your market is hearing this same message and doing the exact same thing. You're not differentiating yourself by showing up in a unique way, or communicating a clear message that sets you apart.

Why do you jump on these bandwagons? To "get more leads" so you can gain more clients.

But what if there were another way to grow your business?

What if you don't need "more leads" to generate more income?

What if you could convert more of the leads you're already generating?

You're spending thousands of dollars every month to make the phone ring. You're getting leads. The question is: How many are you converting?

When you don't convert a lead, you're giving them—and their fee—to your competitor.

I've yet to meet an attorney who couldn't benefit from putting an extra $500,000 in their pocket each and every year by focusing on converting more of the leads they're already generating.

And the beauty is that this doesn't cost you any more advertising money. You're already paying to get the leads to call you. Now you just need to convert more of them into clients.

I (Michael) have helped business owners in a variety of industries, including attorneys, increase their revenue simply by converting more leads into clients. We teach them how to create a unique position in their market. We work within their current advertising channels, never increasing expenses. We help them deliver their message in a such a different and compelling way that prospects bond with them, then hire them.

We teach them the power of *Positioning*.

Positioning is not a new shiny object. It's been around for thousands of years. That's the problem—and the solution.

It's a problem because everyone is looking for the *next new thing*. For some reason, people think new is better. Instead of looking back to see what has worked for others, they look ahead and hope that the next new thing will be the savior of their firm. That's misplaced hope and poor business strategy.

It's the solution because positioning is a proven concept. When embraced and applied properly, it works without fail. It has catapulted more people to expert status than any other strategy known to man.

When I left full-time vocational ministry to start my marketing firm, I knew I needed to differentiate myself from other ad agencies, marketing firms, and media reps. I needed a way to tell my story, capture attention, and get prospects to trust me. I needed a way to position myself uniquely so I would stand out, be different, and generate income.

I used the strategy you will learn in this book to build my business from one client in one town into a highly profitable publishing company serving clients throughout the United States and in two other countries.

I didn't create this concept. But I have polished and simplified it. In these pages you'll learn how to properly position yourself, become known as the *expert* in your market, and use your book to convert more of the leads you're already generating—*without* spending more money on advertising.

Does that interest you? Then I invite you to read with an open mind. Hear what we have to say. Decide if you can use this concept to convert more of the leads you're already generating without spending more money on advertising.

Others have done this. Now it's your turn.

But you don't have to listen only to me. In the next chapter, I invite you to read through a conversation I had with Harlan Schillinger.

Harlan helped to create Network Affiliates, the nation's most prestigious advertising agency for law firms. Harlan is like E.F. Hutton – when he speaks, people listen. And when they follow his advice, they generate more revenue and put more money in their pocket. He's a legend in legal advertising and you would be wise to follow his counsel.

Turn the page and join me in listening to Harlan.

Chapter 2.

Listening to Harlan

Harlan's story

Back in 1974 I moved next door to a gentleman named Bill Muyskens, who was the executive creative director of J., Walter, Thompson, one of the largest agencies in the world. Bill soon expressed to me his desire to leave the agency and fulfill his vision of producing television commercials for upper-end retailers and professional services firms. Key to his model was *syndication*, making one commercial and distributing it to many business. The key was to make very high end, national quality commercials with high production value, so you could go back to back with a national commercial and NOT take a back seat.

Soon he asked me to join the firm of Madison, Muyskens and Jones—the first syndication firm in the United States for professionals in upper-end retail. For instance, we would service fine jewelry stores (like Tiffany's that were not on sale) that wanted to project a strong polished image. We produced commercials that were off the charts.

In addition to developing our syndicated commercials, we continued to produce the spots for Noxzema ("Take it off, take it all off"), Chevy ("Like a rock"), Irish Spring soap, and De Beers diamonds.

In 1979 we recognized that the legal profession was about to explode. Only one lawyer in the country was advertising back then: Len Jacoby from Jacoby and Meyers. He jumped the gun and started advertising prior to the Bates decision (*Bates v. State Bar of Arizona*, a case whose decision by the Supreme Court allowed legal advertising).

Lawyers around the country were soon to start advertising. Opportunity was before us. So we at Madison, Muyskens and Jones added "legal" to our category list. We produced a series of television commercials for legal professionals, and to this day I look back at those commercials and think, "I could probably still run most of them." Now of course we'd have to update the wardrobe to align with current styles, but the concepts were very solid. I give that credit to Bill Muyskens, who was a genius at perceiving the future and understanding the public.

In 1984, my partners were looking to retire soon. But I was a young buck who wanted to press forward. My vision was to expand the company nationally and become a full-service agency. Opportunity knocked at my door in the person of Norton Frickey, the second lawyer to ever advertise. Norton Frickey changed my life. I traveled to Denver to sit down with him, and by the time I left we had decided to merge our business opportunities into his already up and running, Network Affiliates. Our first year working together, Network had seventy clients. The next year it went to eighty clients. Network Affiliates was considered the premier legal advertising agency for Law firms in the United States.

The late 80s were good advertising years. Every commercial we ran lit up the phones. The intake people answered phones and tried to establish rapport. Then I had to face the perennial question: What should I send the prospect after they contact one of my clients? How would I handle *intake and conversion*?

Competitive agencies came on the scene and the dog fight for business really began.

Law practice is a business

If you own a law firm, you should recognize that you are a business that operates on intake and conversion. That is, your business depends on gaining clients, turning those clients into settlements, and turning those settlements into profit. Since you are running a business, you must use business-oriented tactics. Running a law firm is quite similar to running a supermarket, clothing store, sporting goods store, or any other type of a business. You must attract new clients, satisfy them, and keep in touch for the future.

Attorneys receive one hour of training in *the business of law* during law school. Then they are sent out onto the street with absolutely no business sense and no formal education in running a business. No one teaches them how to run a business systematically, professionally, and profitably. They are thrown to the wolves.

The components of marketing

So let me teach you a bit about the marketing side of business. Here's a simple list of the stages of legal marketing:

- Advertising (making the phone ring)
- Engaging callers and visitors
- Intake (using software)
- Appointment setting
- Signing client
- Servicing the client

The first major component of successful legal advertising is *attracting clients*. No matter what line of business you are in, you must attract clients. I bet you spend a lot of time and energy trying to attract clients. And I will tell you that how you deal with each potential client determines your future. In my years of consulting, I have noticed that many lawyers spend thousands of dollars to make the phone ring, but then they drop the ball. They fail to *engage callers and visitors*. They have a cordial conversation with the prospect on the phone—but they never follow up and reengage.

Once your intake person says "Thank you" and hangs up the phone, what happens next? Do you have anything to send the prospect so they remember your call? You cannot rely on your so-called credibility, reputation, and charisma.

The average prospect who has been in an accident calls a minimum of three lawyers within an hour once they sit down with the phone. They want to gather information. Now, they cannot possibly remember every conversation that took place. So you need to put an intelligent marketing piece in front of her soon after—a "leave-behind piece" or "thank-you piece."

Perhaps you send prospects a brochure, a business card, a pen, a thank-you card, a gift card, even a text message. Guess what? Every other firm with a mind for marketing is doing the same thing. Because there's another thing law school doesn't teach you: creativity. Your marketing materials probably look just like your main competitors' marketing materials.

For my clients, I insist that they put something into their prospects' hands that the prospect will *remember* and *use*.

The ultimate business card

That's why I love books. A book is a brochure on steroids. It's your opportunity to communicate with the prospect intelligently, economically, productively, and uniquely. A book is genuinely useful, because you can explain legal matters the prospect needs to know. She will use your book to navigate through her case and then proudly put it on her shelf—especially if you sign it. Do you think your book will end up in the circular file along with your competitors' marketing materials? I think not.

A book makes your follow-up process easier too. You certainly don't want to ignore the prospect after your first conversation. You need to contact her again within a few days. Most attorneys who do this have no excuse for calling other than, "Uh, have you thought about whether you want to do business with me?" As an author, you can ask, "Did you receive the special free copy of my book that we sent to you via two-day mail? Have you read it yet?" The prospect may have spoken to half a dozen competitors since your last conversation. But the book forms the basis of a unique relationship. It's a bridge between you and her. You are giving a gift with substance, knowledge, and personality. Your book is genuinely *helpful*—not another useless brochure about you, you, you.

See, many firms put together a fancy brochure. However, distinguishing your brochure from your competitors' in the eyes of the prospect is almost impossible. Firms include fancy DVDs or a link to online videos, thinking that will "personalize" the brochure. But I'll let you judge: What could be more personal than receiving a book signed to you by the author?

Brochures are perceived as a *selling* piece. It's about selling the law firm. It's about me, me, me: "Look at how great I am! I can help you.

Here's a picture of me in the courtroom, and another taken in my fancy office. Hire me!" Books are perceived as a *teaching* piece. You write a book because you want to *educate* and *help* others. You're a teacher—not a salesman. And you get the credibility of a teacher (instead of the credibility-lack of a salesman). That is the most distinguishable difference between putting a *brochure* out and putting a *book* out: the level of credibility. And credibility helps convert.

Most attorneys I talk to have considered writing a book. But they don't because they think writing a book is a major project—a mountain they simply cannot climb. They lack time. They lack know-how. But as you read this book, you'll see how writing your own book is simpler than you think. And when you are an author, you gain an instant competitive advantage over all the firms in your marketplace.

Do you need more leads?

Speaking at events across the nation, I meet many attorneys. Commonly an attorney shares this problem: "Harlan, I need more leads. I need to grow my business, so I need more leads." That language is a red flag for me. If I ask him to clarify further, he says, "Well, the leads I'm getting really aren't *good* leads. My agency is delivering poor leads." There's the real issue. Personally, I believe every lead is a good lead. Every time your phone rings, every time someone walks into your office, you receive a good lead. Maybe you can do business with them tomorrow if not today.

So to diagnose the attorney's real issue, I ask *What are you doing with the leads you are already getting?* Over the years I have discovered that attorneys want to consume as many leads as possible. Running an ad agency, my least favorite phone calls were from clients complaining that they didn't have enough leads: "Harlan, despite your ads, my phone is not ringing! I'm not getting business." Now, I knew I was making their phone ring. I was delivering those phone calls, but the attorney was unsatisfied. As I dug deeper I uncovered the problem: "Harlan, I guess you are getting me some calls, but they're not *good* calls. So get me more calls."

After many of these conversations I became concerned that my clients were wasting perfectly good leads. We delivered telephone calls, but most of our law office clients were unprepared to make the best of them. I got fed up. Why should I send an attorney more calls if he's not converting his current calls?

So I called time out. I demanded that my clients show me how they handled calls. I began recording every phone call that came into their office and installed accountability software to measure what worked and what didn't.

What do you think I discovered? I found that most of my clients' potential business was falling through a flawed intake system into the cracks. This was my epiphany. From that point on, *understanding intake and lead conversion* was my mission and the focus of my ad agency.

Increasing conversion

Do you want to grow your business? Find ways to convert more clients without increasing your costs of acquisition. Many lawyers simply spend more money and try to buy more leads. But you can take a more intelligent approach: "I am determined to get more business without spending more money." That's the ultimate increase. If you can increase your business by a mere 2% without spending any more money, your net gain is significant.

I love using a book to increase conversions. Why? Because it enables you to have a conversation with your prospect. You hand her an intelligent conversation piece that differentiates you from Bob and Joe down the street. She goes home and relaxes in the evening with—what? Your competitors' brochures? I think not. She's in her favorite easy chair reading *your book*. She's conversing with you at her leisure. Through your book she comes to know, like, and trust you; those are the factors that drive conversion.

What will she do with your book when she finishes it? Throw it away? Never. Nobody throws books away. They have shelf life—literally! When you invest time, energy, and finances into a book, your return on investment continually flows in for decades. Content is timeless. And if you want to address industry changes, simply write another chapter and publish a new edition every few years. Your last marketing campaign expired after a few months. A book is immortal.

Marketing on a shoestring budget

Every law firm has a marketing budget. Yours may be large. It may be satisfactory. It may leave much to be desired. But no matter the size of your budget, you must wisely choose how to spend it. What are the essentials? What are the nice-to-haves? What is simply unnecessary?

I believe there are two things every law firm must have, regardless of budget:

❶ A way for your prospects to find you

❷ Something to send prospects after they find you

The way your prospects will find you today is through your *website.* Anyone who gets in an accident will search Google for the best lawyers around. Your website puts you on the map, broadcasting your existence to anyone looking. This is the beginning of attracting business.

Once your prospects find you, you need a way to engage them. And in a heartbeat, I would choose to send them a book. It's the most impactful item you can put in someone's hands.

If I had a minimal budget and little time, a website and a book are the two main weapons I would utilize. Why? Because no matter whom you speak with, no matter what speech you give, no matter what networking events you attend, people are going to look you up on the Internet—so you need a website. And when all those people find you, you want them to remember you. So you need to give them something to remember you by. Beat the competition by handing out the ultimate business card—your book.

Transactional vs. relational selling

As I mentioned above, in order to send your book to a prospect you must capture their contact information. You now know about them. And they have an easy next step to deepen their connection with you: read your book. It's a low-pressure step toward you. And when they finish reading, they just might be ready to take another step.

See, one of law firms' biggest mindset mistakes is thinking *transactionally.* Lawyers want to sign every caller soon; if they can't, they give up forever. But you know what? Most people don't sign up on the first phone call. The caller wants to shop. He wants to look around. You paid maybe $100 to field his telephone call. What will you do now? You should put his information into a database so you can continually stay in touch with him. That's thinking *relationally*. Maybe his case isn't right for you today, or he isn't ready today. But maybe he'll be ready five years down the road. And because you have stayed in contact through the years, he'll call you.

Getting his information is the initial challenge. However, if you have something to intelligently send him, gathering information will be a whole lot easier. Having that information is vitally important. If you consider social media, it's about databases. Facebook—one of the most valuable companies in the world—is simply a database. It's a gathering of information so that you can continually stay in touch with people. Facebook offers *connectivity* to get you to share your information. How will you convince your prospects to share? How valuable is their information to you?

Thinking relationally, the moment of first contact between you and the prospect is when the relationship begins. You want to connect quickly and stay in front of her longer. Your book is an initial offer with enduring value. It's a relationship-building resource that informs and educates. Your prospect will return to your book, re-reading portions whenever she thinks about legal matters.

The nitty-gritty

Here are several specific ways I would use a book to market your practice:

- ⮩ Send it out. The prime directive of book marketing is send your book to all prospects. Your phone rings every day—make the postal service busy every day. This is a fantastic way to collect callers' contact information. Even callers who like to be anonymous shoppers will identify themselves to get a book. And your book opens a dialogue, quickly and effectively shifting the conversation from how great you are to how you can help the caller.

- ⮩ Business card. A book is the ultimate business card. Unlike your normal business card, which is destined for the trash heap, your book will be placed by your prospect on her desk or shelf or nightstand. Carry books in the trunk of your car to give away, instead of business cards. If you insist on the card, fine—use it to bookmark the most important chapter. Your book grants you far more credibility than a business card.

- ⮑ Speaking handout. Give your book to every single person at any event you attend. Do you speak at the Rotary club? The Better Business Bureau? A local seminar? A regional conference? Make sure every person in the room walks away with your book in his hands.

- ⮑ Website offer. Offer your book on your website. This is a gift people want! They know brochures and info packets are about you trying to sell them. But a good book focuses on the reader: her problems and your solutions. You say, "May I send you my book so you can be better educated about your problem? This book is not about me. It's all about you." On your website, post an easy opt-in form where visitors can input their information. Collect name, email, phone number, and address. You can then communicate value to them through all those channels.

- ⮑ Easy referral. Would you like your clients to refer you to their family and friends more often? Of course you do. The trick is to make it easy and not awkward for your client. A book lubricates any referral opportunity. Give each of your clients two books: one for them, one for a friend. Books are natural conversation pieces. And "read this book my attorney wrote" removes pressure from the conversation. Few people want to give out your business card, but surprisingly many will spread your book around the city.

Think about the psychology behind marketing with your book. Have you ever received a book? How did you feel? Why might you stand in line for the author to sign your copy? Did it make the book any more valuable or personal for you?

Decision-making is not solely intellectual. Your prospects are people with emotions. Most of the time, they use their head to justify what they already want to do in their heart. As your prospect reads your book he will bond with you. He will start *wanting* to hire you. The one-on-one conversation of a book tells your story and connects on a deep level. It starts a relationship. And isn't that what every prospect wants? A lawyer who will care about *them*, not only their case. A lawyer who values relationship as he works to resolve their problem.

The final question

Do you seriously want to increase your income? Publish a book. It's easier than you think with the right help. Publishing is propulsive—it will take you further down the road of marketing success than you ever thought possible.

Chapter 3.

The Solution to Your #1 Problem

So you're generating leads from the advertising and marketing that you're doing. The phone is ringing and you're capturing those leads in your intake system.

> Why are you converting such a small percentage of these calls?
> Why aren't you gaining more clients?
> Why aren't you making more money?

> Your #1 problem is not "getting more leads."
> Your #1 problem is *converting more* of the leads you're already generating.

What's the solution?

Conventional Wisdom

If you talk with other attorneys or people in the media, their solution is to do more advertising.

> Conventional wisdom says that
> by spending more money on advertising
> and filling your funnel with more leads
> you'll get more clients.

There's some truth to that. But I don't think it's the best strategy.

Increasing the sheer volume of leads is not the best answer to your problem. It might work, but it will cost you a lot of money.

If you're advertising properly and your phone is ringing, then you're likely getting enough leads. You need to look at other areas in your business to see where you are losing money. Fill the holes in your bucket and you'll retain more "water" and make more money.

Here are two of the most common holes we find in most firms:

Hole ❶ – Intake

The first place to look is your intake process.

How do your people answer the phone?

- Are they clear?

- Are they friendly?

- Are they inviting?

- Do they put the caller at ease? Or is this caller an interruption for them?

- The person answering your phone is one of the most important people in your firm. They are the first human most people talk with and they set the tone for the rest of the relationship. They are responsible for inviting prospects into a conversation, capturing their information, and making them feel better about your firm than the others they are calling. And your prospects are calling other firms!

You need to train your intake specialists to ensure they are adequately equipped. Chris Mullins and Intake Academy is a great way to do this. Chris wrote the book *Intake Specialists*, and is an expert on intake who can train your law firm staff to excel in this critical area. You can learn more about Chris and her services at intakeacademy.com/

Another expert on the intake and conversion process is Gary Falkowitz, Esq. of Maximum Intake Consulting and Intake Conversion Experts. Gary and his team can help you develop and implement efficient, effective and powerful intake procedures to convert more callers into clients. He can also help if you are looking to outsource your mass torts intake campaigns. You can connect with Gary at www.MaxIntake.com.

> **If you are not maximizing your intake process,**
> **you are marginalizing your revenue.**
>
> Gary Falkowitzl

So now you have generated a lead, have an Intake Specialist answering the phone, and have put the lead into your Intake System.

What you do next makes all the difference.

Hole ❷ – Conversion

Harlan says "intake and conversion is the most overlooked part of your business." So let's fix that.

> Generating a lead is important.
>
> Answering the phone properly is critical.
>
> Inputting them into your system is vital.
>
> *What you send them* after they call is what will convert them from a lead into a client.

You Lose Clients at This Step

What do you send a lead after they call?

Your full color company brochure filled with papers and information about how great you are, how long you've been in business, and how much money you've helped others receive?

- Perhaps a white paper on the topic they called in about?
- Awards you've won or events you've sponsored?
- A picture of your building and staff?

- ⮑ A journal for them to record their thoughts and memories?

- ⮑ And don't forget your refrigerator magnet and business card.

These are all things leads receive when they call an attorney. In fact, since they call multiple firms, they receive piles and piles of this stuff.

It's overwhelming and confusing.

Here's the real problem:

It all looks the same.

Everyone says the same thing.

Change the logo and the color and they would all be identical.

How should the prospect choose whom to hire?

Show up looking like everyone else and you will lose more than you win.

Instead of showing up looking like all of your competitors, do something different. Position yourself uniquely. Don't just send what everyone else sends. Put a **credibility-builder** in your prospect's hands. You will stand out, impact the prospect memorably, and move yourself to the *top* of the pile.

Top-of-the-pile is a great position. And reaching it is easier than you might imagine. But the path of conventional wisdom will lead you astray—that's why you need to follow the pathway of unconventional wisdom.

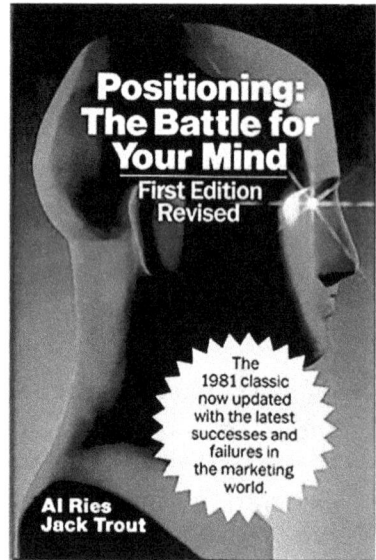

(Un)Conventional Wisdom

In 1981, Al Ries and Jack Trout published their landmark book *Positioning: The Battle for Your Mind*.

Ries and Trout studied dozens of companies, researched endlessly, and discovered the elusive element that made some brands more dominant than others—even when the dominant brand was not as good as its competitors.

Have you read *Positioning*? If not, you need to. But until then, here's how you can apply Ries and Trout's conclusions to your firm.

The Premise

The marketing battle is fought *in the mind of the prospect.*

How people *think about you* is most important. It really doesn't matter if you're the biggest, best, oldest, most experienced, or most advanced.

What matters is your position on the ladder in their mind.

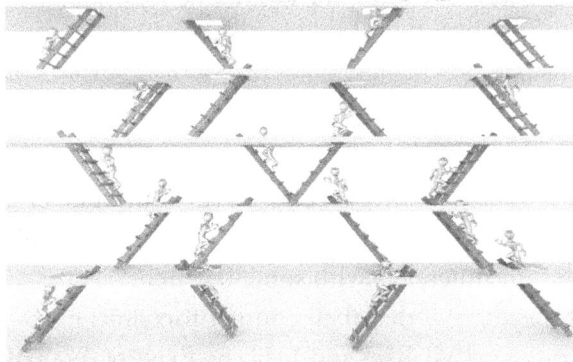

We all have "ladders" in our mind with rungs for every product category. For example, when asked to name a rental car company, most people say **Hertz** first.

Pizza delivery: **Domino's**

Online retailer: **Amazon**

Hertz, Domino's, and Amazon *own* the #1 Position in the mind. That's why they are dominant and earn the lion's share of the business in their category.

The decisive factor is not whether they are better than all their competitors (lots of people prefer Papa John's or Pizza Hut). The decisive factor is that they are the company people **think of first** and **feel the best about**.

These companies obviously can't sit around and allow their business to flounder, or permit their customer service to go down the drain. They still need to continually improve, market, and innovate. But that is much easier to do when you are #1 than when you are barely surviving.

Another company that came to dominate its market is Federal Express. They came onto the scene with a very clear message:

When it absolutely, positively has to be there overnight.

FedEx now owns the word "overnight" in the mind. Is it any wonder why they are the top delivery company in the world?

So positioning works for companies. But can it work for people? Sure it can.

When you think of business growth gurus and motivational experts, who comes to mind?

Tony Robbins is very often the first name mentioned.

Michael Hyatt has burst onto the scene in recent years, positioned as your "Virtual Mentor."

Dave Ramsey has created a fortune by positioning himself as America's personal finance go-to guy.

Now I like Tony and Michael and Dave—but none of them are that much smarter or better than the next guy. In fact, you can get much of what they offer for much less with some research.

But what they have—that their competitors don't have—is **position**.

We see Tony and Michael and Dave as Experts. We trust what they tell us. And we pay handsomely for it.

They have created a platform for their message, generate a large following, and produce shocking profits.

They weren't the first ones to the game. Arguably, they might not even be the best. But they are considered the *experts* in their industries. Since they have this position, they can spend less on advertising, enjoy higher conversions, and generate more revenue.

How to Climb the Positioning Ladder

So how did they create this position for themselves?

What made Tony, Michael, and Dave experts?

They each published a Best Selling Book.

It's that simple.

Tony Robbins came onto the scene with his book *Unlimited Power*. That book made him a national expert and a household name.

Michael Hyatt published *Platform* and it catapulted him to national expert status.

Dave Ramsey published *Financial Peace* in 1992 and has gone on to build a media conglomerate billing millions of dollars a year.

All three of these men were once sitting where you are now, reading someone else's book. They decided to take action and put their thoughts into a book—and the rest is history.

You are an expert in your field. People look to you for advice, counsel, and guidance. You've studied your profession and can discuss it in depth for hours.

You're not missing knowledge.

You're missing **credibility**.

Positioning works for companies and national experts. Will it work for you?

Absolutely.

I've worked with many local experts to position them as the expert in their category.

I give my book to past and current clients, other professionals I work with (i.e. doctors, physiotherapists, chiropractors, etc.), motorcycle shops, schools, shows, and anywhere else I can think of. It is far better than giving out my business card since it shows I care about motorcycle safety and society.

Steve Grover

Grover Law Firm, Alberta, CA
Author, "Ride Hard, Ride Safe"

Within six weeks of our book being published we had someone buy it through Amazon, read it, call to set an appointment, and transfer over $550,000 of assets to our firm.

Michelle Bertram

Author, "Creating Your Dream Retirement"

I'd thought about writing a book, but that was as far as it went. Not knowing the 1st step made it hard to get started. Michael and his Team helped me think of my book as a marketing tool. Every marketing piece you will ever do has a limited shelf life, except your book. When was the last time you discarded a book? The uses available to market my company using my book seem unlimited.

Mike Davidson

Author, "Start Me Up"

I didn't write this book to become a New York Times bestseller. I wrote the book to help my marketing and build my business. The book has accomplished exactly what I wanted it to do—my business has grown drastically.

Lee Welfel

Author, "The Mortgage Book"

What has it done for me? It has probably paid for itself 25 times over or more.

David Lukas

Author, "Whose Future Are You Financing?"

One family was looking at four of my competitors. I gave the wife a book, and she said, "You've written the book on the issue that I'm dealing with! My decision has been made. We're going with you."

Sam Sellers

Author, "Finding Freedom at Home"

People hire lawyers they like and trust. That's one reason I've written so many books. I want people to see me as the expert in my field and the person they can trust to solve their problems.

Ken Hardison

Author, "Systematic Marketing"
President, PILMMA | Legal Marketing Expert

These are just a few of the many business-owner-authors we have helped become experts in their market.

The legal market is ultra-competitive. To stand out and be noticed you need to be recognized as an expert.

You must differentiate yourself and position yourself as *the expert* in your market. This is how fortunes are created.

To do that you need a powerful weapon: your own book.

Your book is the most cost-effective tool in your marketing arsenal. It empowers you to convert more leads and earn more money *without* spending more money on advertising.

When you receive phone calls, don't mail the prospects just your brochure and business card. Send them a signed copy of your book. You'll be the *only* person sending a book—so you will immediately stand out in your prospects' mind.

When they pile all the brochures and business cards they've received onto their table, your book will either be on the *top* of the pile—or **they'll be holding your book in their hand**. Prospects will actually *want* to read your book! It's much more interesting than a brochure. They'll bond with you. They'll trust what you say. They'll see you as the expert they want to hire.

It seems so very simple. Yet so few follow this proven pathway of unconventional wisdom.

When's the last time you threw away a book?

People don't throw away books.
It's almost sacrilegious.

Your book will *stay around longer* than all your competitors' brochures and business cards and miscellaneous junk. Your book will speak to your prospects even when they aren't reading it. Just seeing your book on their table, desk, or nightstand will remind them of you. They'll remember your advice. They'll call you for an appointment.

Do you want to convert more of the leads you're already generating

Your book is the solution to your #1 problem:

converting more leads

and put more money in your pocket without spending more money on advertising? Then you need to position yourself as the expert in your market by becoming the author of your own book.

It's fairly easy to put your name on a book these days. You can publish one yourself (if you have the time). You can license one that someone else has written (a viable alternative). But there's nothing that compares with having your own book that tells your story in your words, especially when you become an Amazon Bestselling Author.

When you are a Bestselling Author, you build an expert platform, easily differentiate yourself, and will have people calling to work with you like never before. Remember Tony, Michael and Dave? This is exactly what they did.

Expert status is the position you need to establish in order to gain more clients without spending more on advertising. And the fastest way to attain expert status is to become a Bestselling Author of your own book.

But why is *this* the best way? Let's find out as we look at how you can use your book to differentiate yourself.

Chapter 4.

How to Differentiate Yourself

> I believe that a book is the ultimate business card. In this competitive market, you either differentiate yourself or you die. Having a book will help you convert leads to clients and put more money in your pocket.
>
> **Harlan Schillinger**
> Legal Marketing Expert

People do business with people they know, like, and trust. Are believe it or not, people hire an attorney primarily because of an emotional decision—not an intellectual one. To gain the emotional trust of the leads you are getting and convert them into clients, you need to spend time with them.

That's why you try so hard to have them set an appointment with you. Whether they visit your office of you go to their home, you know that if you can sit across the table from them, talk with them, and hear their story, they will like you and trust you. And most likely, they will hire you.

The problem is getting them to set an appointment.

What if you were able to have a two-hour conversation with your prospect in the privacy of their home? What if you could have their full, undivided attention? Would that make a difference? Would you be able to convert more leads into clients if you could have a personal conversation with every one of them? The answer, of course, is "Yes!"

This is exactly what you can do with your own book.

We read books by ourselves. When your prospect reads your book, she is attending to no other media…looking at no other competitive brochures…being distracted by no pile of information. You have her undivided attention. And as she turns the pages, she is listening to you. Bonding with you. Believing you.

She is beginning to know, like, and trust you.

You are gaining the credibility that she needs before she will hire you. You are the authority because you wrote the book. She now trusts you.

You have effectively differentiated yourself from every other attorney that she has called. You've positioned yourself uniquely. Everyone else sent her a brochure. You sent her a copy of your bestselling book.

The secret to converting more leads into clients is not to advertise more—but to differentiate yourself by sending every lead a signed copy of your book.

> *Amazon bestselling author status puts you in a category of one in your market, positions you as the expert, and will help you convert more leads into clients without spending more money on advertising.*

Authoring your own book is a wonderful starting point, but you don't have to stop there. To deepen your impact and strengthen your position, you should become an *Amazon bestselling author*.

With the advent of print-on-demand systems, many people can become an author, if they dedicate enough time to it. So having your own book is becoming more commonplace. But being an Amazon bestselling author is rare. Only 1% of the books published ever make Amazon bestseller status.

It is not an easy feat. Promoting a book to Amazon Bestseller Status is a complicated affair. It takes an experienced team, a coordinated promotion strategy, and a lot of time, effort, and energy. But once you become an Amazon bestselling author, this prestigious title will be yours for life—garnering you clients and dollars for the rest of your career.

This is what lawyer Steve Grover does. You can learn a few things from him:

I wanted my book to connect with my market. As a motorcycle enthusiast, I told about my rides, showed pictures of my bikes, and gave helpful information about how to Ride Safe.

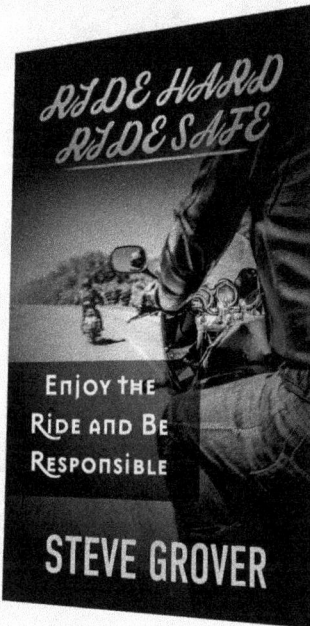

I give my book to past and current clients, other professionals I work with (i.e. doctors, physiotherapists, chiropractors, etc.), motorcycle shops, schools, shows, and anywhere else I can think of. It is far better than giving out my business card since it shows I care about motorcycle safety and society.

Steve Grover
Grover Law Firm, Alberta, CA
Author of *"Ride Hard, Ride Safe"*

Remember what Trout and Ries said about marketing: It is the battle for the mind. When people think rental cars, they think Hertz. When they think pizza delivery, they think Domino's.

You need to position yourself as the number one provider of legal services in the mind of your prospects. Enhance your positioning by becoming the Amazon bestselling author of your own book. Then, when they think "attorney" you are the first one who comes to mind. You will be on the top rung of the attorney ladder in their mind.

Publishing your own book and becoming an Amazon bestseller is the easiest, fastest, and most cost-effective way to differentiate yourself in your market. And because of the increased number of leads you'll convert to clients by using your book, your book not only pays for itself quickly, it continues to generate revenue for years to come.

Tony, Michael and Dave are still earning revenue from their original books. You will use your book for the rest of your career. A small investment today will pays dividends for years.

Let everyone else send brochures and business cards. You send a signed copy of your Amazon bestselling book.

Chapter 5.

How to Convert More Leads

Use your book to convert more leads WITHOUT spending more money on advertising by integrating your book into ALL of your marketing and advertising.

I look at business in 3 Stages:

➲ Attract

➲ Engage

➲ Retain

You can use your book in all 3 Stages of Business and exponentially grow your revenue. We'll discuss these stages in chapter 7. For now, let's focus on the second stage—how to engage and then convert more leads.

After the phone rings and you capture a prospect's information, your Intake Specialist inputs them into your system. Your entire follow up system has to be a well-oiled machine. You must be *fast*. You must be *consistent*. You must be *different*.

Here's one strategy we teach our clients that you can use to convert more leads to clients using your book.

The 4-Step Lead Conversion Process

By follow these steps to deliver a "WOW!" experience to each lead who calls you, you'll convert more leads, gain more clients, and earn more money.

Step 1: If they opt in on your website, give them a call as soon as possible. If they call you, you already have them on the phone. Simply say, "Thank you for considering our firm and requesting some information. Your signed copy of our Amazon Bestselling book [*title*] will be in your hands in two days. We trust this will provide the information you need. Please let us know how we may assist you."

Consider shipping the book via FedEx or mailing it to arrive on the second day. Getting it to them fast will make a big impression.

You'll want to sign the book to them and include other information about your firm and services. You may choose to mail this other information a day or two after mailing the book. This way when they receive your book it's the only thing they get from you that day and it's more likely they'll open it and start reading it.

Direct mail is an effective marketing medium, and the more times prospects receive a package from you the more they will remember you. Plus, your new information will be placed on the top of the pile—always a good place to be. A little more postage could gain you a lot more clients.

Step 2: Call the prospect in 3 days to ask if they have received the book. You want to make sure it was delivered and didn't get lost in the mail.

If it has arrived, say "Great! I hope you enjoy reading it. If you have any questions just let us know."

If it has not arrived, say "I am sorry to hear that. Let me make a note to call you in another day or two. If it hasn't arrived by then, we'll send you another copy."

Step 3: Call them in another 3 days to see if they have read the book. Ask them if they have any questions and/or would like to arrange for a free no-obligation appointment, etcetera.

Step 4: Follow up with them for an appointment as you normally would.

To complement these calls, you should set up a series of automated emails through your preferred email marketing system. By combining the automated emails with your personal calls, you will position yourself as a no-pressure resource who is interested in solving their needs.

It's also a good idea to mail them a personal Thank You card after your first follow-up call with them. How many handwritten Thank You cards do you receive? You will stand out for sure.

This process works wonderfully because it uses multiple media consistently together. Not to mention—it includes a copy of your

Amazon bestselling book. It's also designed to build trust by *not* being like everyone else.

With this simple process you will create expert positioning. You will establish a special position that draws people to you because of your unique status as an Amazon bestselling author and due to your more friendly, low-key, high-touch approach.

Your book and this process will enable you to convert more leads into clients without spending more money on advertising. You'll put thousands of dollars in your pocket year after year without spending more money on advertising. Your book is the one investment that continues to provide a positive ROI the longer you use it.

How else can you use your book? The answer is surprisingly holistic. Turn the page and find out....

Chapter 6.

How to Market as an Author

Converting leads into clients is part of the second stage of business. In this I want you to know that your Amazon Bestselling book will not only help you convert leads—it will also deepen your relationship with existing clients and help you generate more referrals.

The 3 Stages of Business

I define Marketing as:

Everything You Do to GAIN and RETAIN a Client.

Marketing includes generating leads, converting them to clients, and retaining them for life. Most make it more complex than it needs to be. I like to keep it simple.

Every business breaks down into the same 3 Stages. I don't care if you are a mom & pop operation or a multinational conglomerate. At the end of the day all businesses have these same three stages.

The 3 Stages of Business are:

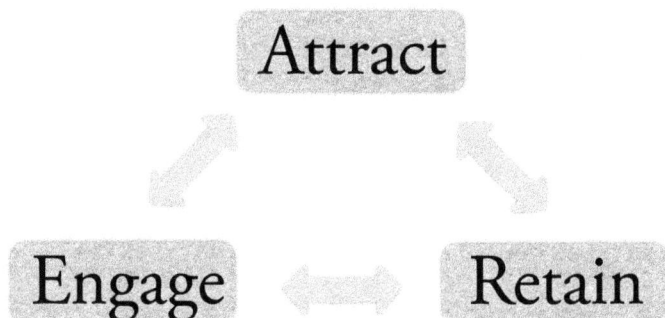

Attract

Engage ⟷ Retain

- Attract – Where most of your money is spent

- Engage – What happens after the phone rings

- Retain – Creating repeat and referral business

How can you use your book to grow your business? By integrating it into each of these 3 Stages of Business.

Attract The ATTRACT Stage is where you are attracting prospects and customers *to* your business. It encompasses how you are perceived in the marketplace by the customer ("positioning"), your reputation, your message, your offers, and even your building's appearance and parking and lighting. All these and more belong to your Attract Stage. It's everything you are doing to attract new customers to your business.

One of the free reports I used to offer was called "The Cheese Report." In it I explained a very simple customer attraction concept that can revolutionize your Attract Stage.

The Cheese Report explained in detail how to get customers to run toward you without reservation: by offering them something they want. I liken it to the "Cat and Mouse Game."

Think about having a mouse in your house. You want him gone. You can either get a good cat to chase the mouse all over the place and hope he eventually catches him…or you can put out some cheese for the mouse and lure him into your trap. Both ways can work. One involves scaring the mouse away, the other attracting him by giving him what he wants.

You want to attract customers. The best way to do that is by giving them what they want—not chasing them all over the place.

In the Attract Stage, you want to consider what your customer is *actually* buying from you. Too many times you only sell features. Or worse yet, you sell the same way as your competitors. You don't want to play that game. Give your customers what they want.

Every year millions of quarter inch drill bits are manufactured and sold.

Would you believe it has been proven that not one drill-bit-purchaser actually wanted to own a drill bit?

The drill bit manufacturer wants to tell everyone about their quality, their steel type, their employees.

All of this falls into the category of "Who cares?"

The customer does not want a drill bit. What the customer wants is a *hole*!

Speak to what your customer is actually paying for. You will attract many more customers and make many more sales.

You can use your book in the Attract stage in a variety of ways. The most common is to offer a free copy of your book on the front page of your website. See how attorney and legal marketing expert Ken Hardison does this on the homepage of his Hardison & Cochran website—http://www. lawyernc.com/.

Ken Hardison
Legal Marketing Expert
Founder of PILMMA

Ken has authored multiple books and he uses them to capture leads, convert clients, and generate revenue. You can do the same when you author your own book.

Ken Hardison is a legal marketing expert. He has built more than one successful law firm, written numerous books on law, and founded PILMMA—one of the country's leading education organizations for personal injury attorneys.

"A book positions you as the authority on the subject matter.

It's a differentiator. It can be used as a lead

magnet, you can also repurpose the content on your blogs, videos and emails. You can use a book in a variety of ways to market your practice.

The big deal is that a book makes you the authority.

People hire lawyers they know, like and trust. They'll trust you more because you're giving them good information."

Engage

Once you have attracted a customer we move into the Engage Stage. This is where your customer begins to connect with you in some way.

Perhaps they visit your website. They might call you. They could even walk through your front door. At whatever point they connect with you, the Attract Stage ends and the Engage Stage begins.

Make certain what you tell your prospects in the Attract Stage matches—or is exceeded by—what your prospects experience in the Engage Stage. Otherwise you'll deliver a bad customer experience. They'll run away...and take their friends with them.

Haven't we all had the experience of hearing about a new restaurant in town? (No offense to restaurant owners.) The restaurant boasts of how wonderful its food and service is. So you go there for dinner, only to experience a noisy atmosphere, small portions of adequate food, and servers who are too busy doing other things to care for your needs.

How likely are you to return?

How likely are you to tell your friends to go there?

That's what happens when your Attract and Engage Stages are not in sync.

Many of the clients I work with have a pretty good Engage Stage when I meet them. You probably do too. That's because it's what you primarily do. The Engage Stage deals with the operational aspects of your business. It's how you deliver your product or service to your customers. It's the core of your business (from a functional standpoint), and it's where you have invested much of your time, effort, and resources.

But there are always ways to improve your Engage Stage. These strategies are a hidden gold mine that many business owners overlook. Don't make that mistake. You need to look carefully at how you engage with your customers and make certain you are delivering what they really want.

> ## Forget about the drill bit.
> ## Focus on the hole!

Using your book in the Engage stage is powerful. The Lead Conversion Process we discussed in the previous chapter details how to use your book to convert a lead into a client in this stage. This is only one of many strategies we teach our clients to help them convert more leads into clients without spending more money on advertising.

Retain

Now we come to the Retain Stage. This is where most business owners fail. And that's unfortunate, because the Retain Stage is where business wealth is created. It's where you retain customers for life, gaining their repeat and referral business.

In the Retain Stage, you build an on-going relationship with your customer. You send Thank You notes for their purchase; you call them; you send them newsletters; you invite them to special events; you give them special offers and exclusive benefits.

You make them feel special—because they are special. They are your customers! They have purchased your product or service. Don't ever allow them to feel like an unloved and uncared—for orphan.

The Retain Stage can become one of the most profitable stages in your business. The customer to get to purchase from you again is a satisfied customer. It takes 7–10x more money to attract a customer than it does to retain a customer.

This is the *least* expensive portion of your marketing mix. Here you can make the biggest impact with the least amount of money—because the "prospects" already know you. You are often the incumbent provider. So keep in touch and nurture a lifelong relationship with them.

Billions and billions of dollars are never generated, never realized…simply because of the neglect or absence of an Retain Stage in most businesses. Examine your Retain Stage, especially the nurturing of lifelong relationships as "repeat business insurance."

That's really what relationship nurturing accomplishes, right? You make sure that when your current client has a need, *they think of you first.* More often than not they will use you again—and not be tempted to try someone else just because they're being offered a lower price.

The Retain Stage is not only for repeat business but also where you gain referral business. Some business owners are under the illusion that much of their business comes from referrals. Occasionally someone comes in and says that a friend referred them, so the business owners assume this is the norm. But referrals are frequently lower than you think. (Just track where your customers are coming from.)

There are three types of referrals:

- Passive

- Reactive

- Choreographed

Let's look at each of these in brief. You will then have a better idea of how to take full advantage of the Retain Stage by maximizing referrals to grow your business.

Passive referrals are when somebody calls you up and says, "Hey, my brother just used your company and he said I should give you a call."

Passive referrals happen without you doing anything to make them happen.

Reactive referrals are when somebody calls up and says, "Hey, my brother John is thinking about getting a new air conditioner, you should give him a call."

Reactive referrals are when you have to react and do something to make them happen.

Choreographed referrals are when you have trained your customers to notice any conversations they have *about your business category* and purposefully introduce you into that conversation.

Your customers endorse you and transfer the trust they have in you to their friends.

> Choreographed referrals are when your customers notice conversations that are about you and introduce their friends to you.

To grow your business quickly, invest some focused effort on your Retain Stage and you'll begin seeing your profits go straight to the bottom line.

One strategy we teach in the Retain Stage is to stimulate referrals from happy clients. Instead of asking them to hand your business card to someone, we teach you a script that endears them to help you serve more people. Then you give them 3 copies of your book to hand out to their friends and you replenish these as they do. It's a powerful referral strategy and a low-cost way to use your book to gain more clients.

You will use your book in all 3 Stages of Business. By increasing each Stage by 10%, you'll increase your business by 33%. It won't happen overnight, but it can happen in the next few months.

National brands like Tony Robbins, Dave Ramsey, and Michael Hyatt have built their platform over time. Today they generate massive revenues and are seen as The Expert in their field. You can do the same.

Chapter 7.

Amazon Awaits – Now Is Your Time

Becoming an Amazon Bestselling Author is not easy. There are a variety of factors that have to be managed, manipulated, and aligned. The promotion sequence and sheer volume required to move any book to bestseller status is staggering.

That's why very few books ever attain it.

Fortunately, we know exactly what to do. When you decide to become an Amazon Bestselling Author, you get more than just that title for life. Here's everything you receive with our program:

❶ Your Own Book

We work with you to create and publish your own book easily and quickly through a series of telephone interviews with our team.

Then your book will be on Amazon, Kindle, and in your hands. This is not some off-the-shelf pre-written book. This is your book that conveys *your message* to *your audience*.

❷ Guaranteed Amazon Bestselling Author Status

We promote your book aggressively to make you an Amazon Bestselling Author—*Guaranteed!*

This prestigious title enhances your credibility, positions you as the expert, and draws people to you magnetically.

❸ 300 FREE Copies of Your Book

We'll send you 300 Copies of Your Book to use to convert more leads.

We'll even teach you what to do with these books to attract leads, engage prospects, and retain clients.

❹ Free Expert Coaching

Our **Expert Coaching Program** teaches you exactly how to use your book to convert more leads, gain more clients, and grow your revenue.

You get 2 Months Free. That's 8 weekly phone calls with your Personal Expert Coach. Think of it as the *Bestselling Author Bootcamp.*

❺ On-Demand Book Orders

Order physical copies of your book to give out for only $5.00 per copy + shipping. This is the least expensive high-impact tool in your marketing arsenal. You control **when** you order, **how many** you order, and **where** you ship them. They'll arrive in just 2–3 weeks.

Or choose our auto-fulfillment plan to have books arrive on your doorstep every month.

Here's how to begin.

Call Michael
(501) 539-0038

Email Michael
Michael@PaperbackExpert.com

Schedule a call with Michael
www.PaperbackExpert.com/PersonalInjury

Bonus:

10 Practical Action Steps

Dear future author,

I'm thrilled that you have taken this step to more fully understand how publishing your own book can help you grow your business. Having a book proudly displayed in your office instantly establishes you as an Authority, increases your Credibility and positions you as an Expert. And most everyone wants to do business with an expert!

There are dozens of ways you can use a book to grow your business. In the following pages I have distilled for you the 10 Ways to Grow Your Business With Your Own Book

Over the next few minutes, you'll learn what other successful business owners, CEOs and business gurus know… how to grow your business by establishing yourself as an expert. It all begins when you publish your own book.

To Your Growth,

Michael

Michael W. DeLon
President, Paperback Expert

❶ Create Customer Loyalty

Every business owner knows that it costs 7 to 10 times more money to gain a new customer then it does to retain a customer. What are you doing to retain customers?

The most profitable companies around the world enjoy having the most loyal customers. Have you heard of the Pareto principle? This is where 80% of your results come from 20% of your efforts. Using that as a standard, we oftentimes find that 80% of tax dollars are paid by 20% of the taxing population. Or, that 20% of your clients make up 80% of your profit.

That being the case, what are you currently doing to thank your best customers? How about giving them a copy of your book? Books make great client gifts and are a terrific customer retention tool. A book is a wonderful tool to create client "stickiness."

Not only does the book communicate thoughtfulness on your end, it also provides a perfectly scripted message to get in front of your clients, and their friends. Your book is a great customer thank you strategy and a superb way to help you retain and build customers for life.

❷ Differentiate Yourself in the Market

What makes the best companies in the world different from everybody else? Think about Disney. What makes Disneyland or Disneyworld stand head and shoulders above every other theme park on earth? For Disney is cleanliness.

People go to Disney and are amazed at how clean the park is. They have a wonderful time and build great memories. And then, when they go home, they tell their friend about the experiences they had, and they always talk about Disney's cleanliness. How clean the park is? Yes! That is a difference maker for Disney. And it's the differentiating factor that has made Disney millions and millions of dollars.

In today's crowded environment it is more difficult than ever to stand out in a crowd and differentiate yourself from everyone else. Did you know that there the over 6,000,000,000 people on Earth, but only about 3,000,000 who are published authors? Becoming an author puts you in the top .05% of people in the world. As an author you gain instant credibility in the eyes of your customers, the media and even your competitors.

- What are you doing to differentiate yourself so that your prospects choose you over every other option they have available?
- What is it that makes you unique?
- How are you positioning yourself and your company to exceed the expectations of your customer?

Being an author tells your prospects that you have taken the time and have made the investment to go the extra mile—and that'll pay for itself time and time again.

Going that extra mile is, many times, just enough to tip the scales in your favor and send a flood of new customers your way. Being an author is the easiest way to differentiate yourself in a very crowded marketplace.

Are you going to take that step and position yourself above the crowd like Disney has, or will you wait for one of your competitors to get there first and play "catch-up" for the rest of your life?

❸ Generate Quality Referrals

What percentage of your business comes from referrals? Truth be told, it is far less than you would like to believe.

Studies have shown that approximately 20% of your customers will refer you to others. Another 20% won't give referrals at all. That leaves 60% who probably would refer you, if you'd only ask and make it easy for them to do so.

The most profitable companies report over 70% of new customers come from referrals. And with the cost of advertising and marketing continuing to go up while not producing adequate results, referrals are your best and most cost effective marketing tool.

Smart business owners give a copy of their book to every customer and ask them to hand them out to their friends, neighbors, relatives and business associates. This immediately increases your sphere of influence without costing you much money at all.

Publishing a book instantly creates a "conversation starter" with customers and their friends. You've just made it super easy for your best customers to refer you to their friends – who are people just like them.

The other big deal here is that when they give out your book, you control the message being sent.

No one can tell your story better than you. Without a book, you never know what may be said about you. With your book in their hands, you are 100% certain that your message will be delivered exactly as you desire every time.

Give copies of your book to your best customers and ask them to simply pass those along to others. Doing this ensures that you control 100% of the message and you'll expand your influence more quickly for much less cost.

❹ Get Free Media Coverage

What's the fastest way to get local news media to look at your business and feature you in newspaper, on TV and radio?

Almost every business owner would love to be featured in a magazine or on TV, but for most that remains just a dream. The media doesn't care about you; they only care about delivering good content to their audience. They want a great story; and your book can be a great story.

Being an author makes you an expert. It also makes you a credible source. Reporters are constantly looking to interview experts for their stories. Publishing a book positions you in the eyes of the media favorably, and puts you on the top of their list as a place to go for comment and opinion for future articles and interviews.

Whether you are talking about TV, radio, newspaper or online coverage, being an expert will get you noticed, and then it will get you more business. Would you like to be running a monthly article in your largest trade journal? Your book could be your ticket in.

If you desire to grow your business, becoming a darling of the media is a great way. To do that, you need a story. That story is your book. The old adage is truer now than ever before:

Publish or perish.

❺ Attract New Customers

As a business owner, you always have to be attracting new customers. But instead of chasing after customers using the traditional methods, what you want to become is a customer attraction magnet. You need to develop what we call a "lead generation magnet" for your company. You want to attract customers to you so that you don't have to chase after them.

Your book can be your lead generation magnet. Would you like to give a book to all of your customers and best prospects that would immediately point them back to doing business with you? That book is your book.

Let me show you an example. Carl Sewell is the CEO of Sewell Automotive in Dallas Texas. In 1990 Carl published a book titled, "Customers for Life."

Every prospect that walked into a Sewell Cadillac dealership received a complimentary copy of Mr. Sewell's book, even if they were "just looking." Well, as you can imagine, many of those prospect read, or at least glanced through, that book and learned of Sewell's 10 Commandments of Customer Service. After reading the book they realized they wouldn't receive that type of service anywhere else, and they chose to purchase their vehicles from Sewell.

Interestingly enough, in 1991 when Sewell published his book, he had three dealerships in Dallas. Today, Sewell has over 20 dealerships scattered around Dallas, Fort Worth, San Antonio and the surrounding areas. Do you think his book had anything to do with his success and growth?

❧

How can you leverage your book to acquire new clients?

First, hold a Book Signing Party and give a personally signed copy of your book to your best customers and prospects.

Second, hold a client appreciation party and provide a complimentary copy of your book as a gift.

Third, mail or personally deliver a copy of your book to every client who does not attend your appreciation party.

Fourth, give a copy of your book to key influencers in your community, along with organizations and associations you are affiliate with.

Fifth, offer your book for free on your website. You'll need to capture their name and mailing address in this process, which will allow you to send other materials to them in the future.

Finally, if you have a retail business, give a copy of your book to every serious customer who enters your doors. If Carl Sewell can do it, why can't you?

❻ Message Multiplication

Business owners are busy people, always having too much to do and too little time. How in the world are you supposed to get your message out to so many people?

A book allows you to be in multiple places at once. Like mass media, publishing a book gives you greater coverage in less time (and for a much smaller investment than traditional media channels). You should be actively looking for, and taking advantage of, the most profitable distribution channels available to you. Your book is a great channel to deliver your message exactly as you desire.

Publishing a book allows you to leverage your time by talking with multiple people at the same time. You can give it to people at meetings, social clubs, at the country club or at an event. Even in an elevator when you have even less time, instead of handing them your business card, give them a copy of your book.

If you want to take your business to the next level, you need to work smart, not just hard. Multiply yourself through the power of publishing your own book. It's the best way to multiply your message and grow your business.

❼ Your Most Cost-Effective Marketing Tool

What's the most cost effective marketing that you do?

Publishing your own book can be the most cost effective marketing that you ever do. A book is one of the most powerful marketing tools in a small business owner's arsenal, and oftentimes, the most cost effective.

Do you know your cost per lead? What about your cost per client? Most small business owners don't know these numbers. Unless you are really tracking and managing your return on investment your marketing efforts are most likely woefully underperforming… and you'll never know why.

Your book is an image advertisement, a business card, a direct response advertisement and a terrific credibility builder all in one. For about 5 dollars per unit or less, your book can do a lot of heavy lifting for your business.

A book is a phenomenal tool to explain the small technicalities of your product or service, or the uniqueness of your business. Your book will most likely become your most effective marketing tool.

As marketing expert Bill Glazer once said,

"It's not that you're going to get rich [from selling your book]…but you can get rich because of it."

❽ Increase Sales Without Salespeople

Would you like to know a secret? This is how smart business owners increase sales without any more salespeople. There are only a couple of ways to grow your business. First, acquire new customers. Second, do more business with a customer you already have.

With that said, would you be interested in a proven way to increase your sales without adding sales people? Publish your own book.

Your book allows you to be in multiple places at the same time. It allows you to have a personal conversation with multiple people without you even being there. When a customer or prospect is reading your book, they are focused solely on you and your message, making it a lot easier to make that sale.

Savvy marketers will also include direct response techniques, bounce back pieces, and special offers within their book to keep the phone ringing and the new lead pipeline full. A book is a cost effective direct response marketing tool that when used properly will turn on the flow of new leads, help you increase sales and grow your revenue without adding overhead or salespeople. Best of all, books don't take 2-hour lunches nor do they talk back or call in sick.

Publishing a book is your fast track to increase sales without hiring salespeople.

⑨ Your Ultimate Business Card

What does your business card look like and how do you use it? I think your business card should be your book.

When you meet a prospect, what's the first thing you do when you sit down in person? You hand them your business card, right? I want you to start thinking about handing them a copy of your book instead. Using your book as your business card in your initial meeting changes the entire dynamic of your meeting and relationship.

You could say something like this,

"Mr. Prospect, thank you so much for spending a few minutes with me today. I really appreciate you making time to meet with me. As a small token of my appreciation, I would you like for you to have a copy of my latest book. I think you will really enjoy it."

Now when you say that, two *big* things will normally happen:

First, your prospect will sit up in his chair and take great interest in everything else you have to say. As an Author, your status in their eyes immediately goes up. You must be an expert!

Second, your prospect will now be pre-sold on you before you even open your mouth. Why? Because your book is the ultimate sales letter or brochure and it sells the prospect on why you are the expert and why they should do business with you.

Rather than handing them your business card from across the table, start handing them a copy of your book. You'll begin to see big changes in how you are perceived, and more importantly, in your sales.

Your book will be the most profitable business card you've ever created.

⑩ Generate More Leads

Use your book to build your email list. Most every company has an email list they are trying to build. Most do this from a simple sign up at their website or via Facebook.

I recommend that you use your book to generate more names for your email list. Offer to send your book free of charge to anyone who is interested. You may want to pre-qualify them a bit, or ask them to pay a small shipping and handling fee to help defray the cost. If they're a good prospect and are really interested in what you provide, they'll be willing to part with a few dollars to get your book. It's really a "no brainer", especially since a book has real perceived value.

This process will help you to identify them as a key prospect, and now you have their name and contact information so you can follow up with more specific and targeted direct mail. Perhaps you could send them a company brochure, or invite them to an upcoming event are make them some other special offer that you have.

Using your book to build your mailing list is a great way to increase your sales and grow your business. This will also result in lowering your cost per lead and cost per sale.

Special Offer

- How much would you pay to have a 30-minute personal conversation with Harlan Schillinger?

- I'll let you eavesdrop on a private conversation I had with Harlan about Legal Marketing. The insights I gained have been worth thousands to me. They'll be worth tens of thousands to you. (Value = Priceless)

- Ken Hardison's – Systematic Marketing ($17.95 Value)

- Michael's first book – On Marketing, The Definitive Guide for Small Business Owners. ($9.95 Value)

- Lead Conversion Strategy Consultation ($250 Value)

- A private 30-minute phone call with Michael to discuss how you can convert more of the leads you are already generating without spending more money on advertising.

- The Automated Marketing System ($399 Value)

- A Step-by-Step Plan to Follow Up with Callers and Convert them to Clients

Over **$597** of Value is Yours FREE
at HowToConvertCallersIntoClients.com.

About the Authors

Michael DeLon is the founder of Paperback Expert.

He's an author, marketing strategist, and business growth coach who specializes in helping small business owners build trust as they position themselves as *The Expert* by publishing their own book. Then Michael teaches them how to use their book to Attract, Engage, and Retain customers for life while stimulating referrals.

He's a straight shooter with over 25 years of experience studying, applying, and fine-tuning these marketing strategies. His vast experience allows him to find unique solutions to his clients' challenges that others never see.

Marketing doesn't have to be a gamble. Michael can help you build trust through authorship and become a recognized expert by publishing your own book!

Michael is the husband of one and father of four. He's a committed follower of Jesus Christ and is deeply involved in his church. You can normally find Michael investing time with his family or helping others grow in their marketing and their marriage relationship.

Reach Michael:
Michael@PaperbackExpert.com

Harlan Schillinger

Old School Ethics; Aggressive Representation

"I start my days and base my relationships trying to establish a fair and equal exchange of value," says Harlan Schillinger.

Harlan is a 38-year veteran of the advertising industry who joined Network Affiliates (www.netaff. com) in 1985 to lead its marketing efforts. Network Affiliates currently represents over 88 clients in over 96 markets. It is considered the pioneer and premier advertising agency for legal advertising and marketing.

Prior to joining Network Affiliates, Harlan was vice president and one of the founding partners of Madison, Muyskens & Jones in Lakeville, Connecticut. Along with his partners, Harlan founded the first syndication firm for retailers using television commercials throughout the United States.

Knowing his clients' businesses and searching out opportunities for them is one of Harlan's strongest agendas. Throughout the year, he attends conventions, speaks at attorney meetings, and participates in prominent roundtable forums throughout the country to help his clients stay on top of the legal field. He is deeply involved with the National Trial Lawyers Summit, 360 Advocate, and PILMMA.

"Creating opportunities and increasing market share for my clients is my No. 1 priority in this tough economy," he says.

Harlan is an avid motorcycle enthusiast who enjoys being a member of the most unique and prestigious custom motorcycle club in the world—the Hamsters USA. His passions are building and riding custom motorcycles and trying to playing golf. Harlan also sits on the Board of the Children's Care Hospital and School in South Dakota (www.cchs. org), a hospital dedicated to helping special needs children.

Reach Harlan:

HarlanSchillinger@gmail.com

www.ingramcontent.com/pod-product-compliance
Lightning Source LLC
Chambersburg PA
CBHW050125240326

41458CB00122B/1422